ideals® CHRISTMAS

I have always thought of Christmas
as a good time;
a kind, forgiving, generous, pleasant time;
a time when men and women
seem to open their hearts freely; and so I say,
God bless Christmas!

—CHARLES DICKENS

IDEALS PUBLICATIONS
NASHVILLE, TENNESSEE

Christmas Comes But Once a Year

Edgar A. Guest

God grant ye joy this Christmas day;
May every heart be jolly;
Love kiss ye now beneath the bough
Of mistletoe and holly.
The long, hard year of toil is done;
Today the bells are ringing.
Put down your burdens every one,
And share the carol singing.

For Christmas comes but once a year,
When harvesting is ended;
With merry din, the day comes in
By love and mirth attended;
The children dance and shout with glee;
The eyes of all are beaming;
And high above the Christmas tree,
The star of hope is gleaming.

So homeward turn your steps once more,
And give a kiss to Mother;
Let horn and bell the glad news tell
Of each returning brother.
For man has conquered time and space,
Regardless of the weather;
And Christmas Day, by God's good grace,
Should find us all together!

At Christmas all roads lead home.

—MARJORIE HOLMES

Lititz Train Station in Pennsylvania.
Photograph by Fred Habegger/Grant Heilman

A holly wreath with bright red, frosted berries
Greets me as I near the waiting door.
I seem to hear the sound of sleigh bells ringing—
It's Christmas Eve, and I am home once more.
—LAURA HOPE WOOD

Homecoming Hearts
D. A. Hoover

At Christmastime when hearts are warm,
As sheltered from the winter storm
We gather at our Christmas tree,
God's love is there, as meant to be.

Though filled with gifts, good food, and fun,
Deep in the soul of every one
Abides the Babe of Bethlehem,
Down to the youngest one of them.

Though years bring changes and paths will stray,
There shines that star each Christmas Day;
Earth knows no paths mankind may roam
Too far from memories of home.

Christmas at Melrose
Leslie Pinckney Hill

Come home with me a little space,
And browse about our ancient place;
Lay by your wonted troubles here,
And have a turn of Christmas cheer.
These sober walls of weathered stone
Can tell a romance of their own;
And these wide rooms of devious line
Are kindly meant in their design.
Sometimes the North Wind searches through,
But he shall not be rude to you.
We'll light a log of generous girth
For winter comfort, and the mirth
Of healthy children you shall see
About a sparkling Christmas tree.

Christmas Baking

Darlene Kronschnabel

Christmas came early to our country kitchen. It arrived with the teasing fragrance of holiday baking drifting through the house; then it went out the kitchen door in the form of festive fruitcakes, tins of Christmas cookies, and holiday breads.

Even before the Thanksgiving dishes were dried and put away, Mother began planning her mincemeat, fruitcake, and cookie baking. She dusted off her heirloom recipe file and pulled out butter-stained newspaper clippings, recipe cards sticky with molasses, and the honey-and-sugar-crusted notes from family and friends. She hunted up her green-handled cookie cutters and lined up baking supplies.

When I was in grade school, World War II was a factor in every event, even Christmas baking, because supplies were rationed or scarce. By managing our sugar allotment and using maple and corn syrup wherever possible, Mother saved enough for her baking.

For the next several weeks she spent all her time in the kitchen. The sweet scents of cinnamon, ginger, nutmeg, cloves, allspice, cardamom, peppermint, chocolate, molasses, vanilla, and almond combined with the flurry of holiday activity to fill our entire family with the Christmas spirit.

The day after Thanksgiving, Mother prepared a batch of spicy-sweet mincemeat and set the mixture aside in a crock to mellow.

"Good things take time," she told me.

Christmas baking officially began when Mother brought out the containers of sticky candied fruit, red and green candied cherries, dried fruit, nuts, and fragrant spices for fruitcake.

Mother believed in traditional fruitcake and enjoyed baking it, perhaps a bit more than we enjoyed eating it. Most of the time, it turned out heavy as lead, or as gummy and flavorless as the ones sold in the store. While we managed to slowly eat them, we did drop more than a few hints along the way. But she had a sense of humor, especially when a young man noticed her gathering fruitcake supplies.

"I always thought there was only one fruitcake in existence, and it just keeps getting passed around every Christmas," he said.

"I'll pretend I didn't hear that," Mother replied. "Someone always brings up that old joke. This year I've made some adjustments, and it's the best recipe I've found." And she was right. We've been enjoying her special fruitcake recipe ever since.

With the mincemeat and fruitcake mellowing, cookie madness hit our country kitchen.

"Christmas wouldn't be Christmas without cookies," Mother insisted. Dad, with his sweet tooth, agreed.

Each day while I was in school, Mother stirred, mixed, and baked peanut butter balls, toffee bars, butterscotch creoles, jelly tarts, poppyseed cookies, red and green kaleidoscope crisps, and molasses-laced gingerbread cutouts. Best of all, she made my favorites: buttery sugar cookies, in all sizes and shapes.

In the evening we sat around the table frosting and decorating what seemed like dishpans full of cookies. When we finished, a dazzling array of stars, bells, wreaths, trees, angels, and Santas lined the kitchen counter. Overnight, they disappeared into storage tins Mother lined up on the basement shelves next to the mincemeat and fruitcake.

There they sat until several days before Christmas, when we brought them back up to the kitchen. Then began the fun of packaging the holiday goodies into special containers to give to friends, neighbors, cousins, aunts, and uncles. And each carried a message: "Merry Christmas from our country kitchen to yours."

A selection from SEASONS IN A COUNTRY KITCHEN

Holiday Aroma
Ruth H. Underhill

There's something about the kitchen
These past few busy days;
It has a special aroma,
More wonderful in many ways.

It seems to be the favorite room
Of everybody here;
It must be the fragrant odor
This holiday time of year.

See the plum pudding bubbling;
Smell the sweetness of spice.
Of all the times of all the year,
Christmastime is oh, so nice!

Over near the cozy fire,
We're busy cracking nuts;
Sister hums a Christmas carol
As candied fruit she cuts.

The cookie jar is brimming;
I just went to take a peek,
But with Mother watching ever so close,
There's not a chance for one to sneak.

Mother keeps opening the oven door,
Popping goodies in and out;
All this can only mean one thing:
Christmas is near, without a doubt!

No Calendar Needed
Lolita Pinney

For many years a calendar
Hung on our kitchen wall,
And Mother checked the busy days
And seasons as they'd fall;
But no calendar was needed
To know the time of year—
By the fragrance of her kitchen
I knew the season near.

True, no calendar was needed
For an eager child to know
That Christmastime was coming!
Mother hurried to and fro
Making special sugar cookies
And our maple sugar candy;
While she whistled Christmas carols,
We knew everything was dandy.

Gingerbread men in the pantry
And fruitcakes in the jar
Teased our noses every minute—
Christmas could not be far!
We cracked nutmeats on the flatiron
And strung popcorn for the tree,
And every hour was heaven
In the kitchen, it seemed to me.

Mother in her big white apron
With some flour on her cheek
Is the dearest recollection
Of my cherished Christmas week.
A calendar was useless;
There was no need for guessin',
For we always knew it was Christmas
By the fragrance of our kitchen.

A country-styled living room. Photograph by Jessie Walker

Come Home with Me for Coffee

Marjorie Holmes

You leave the chaos of cookie baking to wash the baby's face, stuff him into wraps, and, changing to lipstick and heels yourself, dash off to the school program.

Carrying him through a chorus of angels and grinning, bathrobed wise men, you make your way into the auditorium, where in the back rows await the familiar faithfuls who always come.

"Here, I can see better," someone says as you sit down. "Let me hold him on my lap."

Children in the rows ahead beam fondly on the baby and giggle when, spying a brother, he screeches his name and claps. . . . There is the nostalgic scent of pine branches mingling with that of crayons, books, and chalk. A radiator hisses. The children's voices rise shrill and sweet in the ancient carols that take you back . . . back.

"Come home with me for coffee," you impulsively invite your neighbors—and a dear friend whom you haven't seen in weeks. "The house is a mess but it'll be fun to talk."

A light snow is falling as you emerge. It makes a frail dusting on the porch and has already softly furred the handlebars of a bicycle standing at the steps. "Looks like we may have a white Christmas!" people exclaim.

The house looks tumbled but inviting as they cheerfully shed their wraps. The fragrance of your baking makes them sniff.

"What smells so good?" they ask. Snatching at papers and tops, you put the kettle on, while a friend starts a fire in the fireplace.

It is going merrily by the time you return. . . . the fire joins the laughter and the conversation, snapping and crackling in a bright shout. You dart onto the porch to get another log. The snow still falls. Inside are the sounds of your friends. The cookies are crisp and rich, the coffee strong and hot.

House in Lane County, Oregon. Photograph by Steve Terrill

Be merry all, be merry all;
With holly dress the festive hall;
Prepare the song, the feast, the ball,
To welcome Merry Christmas.
—WILLIAM ROBERT SPENCER

Christmas Flower
Gladys Harp

Poinsettia, Christmas flower,
How you flaunt your gorgeous head,
Crowned by leafy coronet,
Brilliant ruby, Christmas red,

Carried high like torches flaming,
Lighting up the Advent time,
Heralding the Christ Child's coming
While your candles skyward climb.

Like a burning Yule log's flame,
You light up the darkest room,
Chasing out the lurking shadows,
Banishing the deepest gloom.

Poinsettia, Christmas flower,
May you live long in fact and rhyme,
Accentuating Christmas spirit
Throughout the holy Advent time.

Holly and Pine
Margaret E. Sangster

When Christmas comes with
        mirth and cheer
To clasp the circlet of the year,
Then forth we go for holly and pine,
Our wreaths of evergreen to twine;
Then swift we trip across the snow
To find the gleaming mistletoe;
And straight and tall and branching free,
We haste to choose the Christmas tree.

A Christmas Wish
Roy Z. Kemp

Light the tall and shining candles;
Hang the bunch of mistletoe;
Place the wreath of berried holly
On the door where it will show.

Deck the Christmas tree with tinsel;
Hang each silver or golden ball,
Ornament of green and yellow,
Red and blue, so none will fall.

Light the hearth fire; let the Yule log
Brightly burn to glowing embers;
Sing the joyous Christmas carols
Which each happy heart remembers.

In homes before a flickering hearth,
Good families gather round
Where warmest Yuletide wishes ring,
Where peace on earth resounds.
—LON MYRUSKI

A rainbow of poinsettias. Photograph by William H. Johnson

Christmas Decorations

Dori Sanders

Aunt Vestula decorated our house for the holidays with the same ritualistic fervor as when she cooked.

She would get my daddy to cut a perfect cone-shaped cedar tree and bring it into the living room. First she placed a wisp of field cotton near the base of each branch. Nobody else in Filbert, South Carolina, put their cotton on the tree that way. Everybody else put it on the outer tips of the branches, but Aunt Vestula tucked it all the way down by the trunk.

Next she went outdoors and gathered small branches from other cedar trees, choosing those with the most dusty, silvery-blue cedar berries. She would tie these little branches onto the tree, along with pine cones and some sprigs of holly with glossy, spiky leaves and bright red berries. Then she would take short lengths of old, used lace—never longer than a yard—and drape them over a few branches. She would cover the ends of the lace with big bows made of white crepe paper, shredding the streamers that trailed from the bows with a fork, to make ribbons.

For the finishing touch, Aunt Vestula polished dried honey-locust pods to a beautiful mahogany color, threaded them onto a string, and festooned the branches with them. My sister Virginia follows this tradition to this day.

Aunt Vestula placed additional sprays of cedar branches, pine cones, and holly with berries all over the house—on and above the mantel, in every window, and even in small wooden kegs.

Finally, Aunt Vestula tied streamers cut from crisply starched gingham and calico cloth around the stair railings, with bows attached here and there from top to bottom, a custom she brought from South Carolina's Low Country, where she worked. Only then was the house ready for the holidays.

Stairwell filled with holiday decorations.
Photograph by Jessie Walker

Christmas tree and hearth. Photograph by Jessie Walker

The Tree
Ruth B. Field

The balsam stood in the darkened room
While the old clock ticked the night away;
Pungent the scent in the stove-warmed gloom,
And the moon looked in at the bright array
Of tinsel festooned there in the dark.
Baubles and candles quivered a bit,
Touched by the moonbeams' silver spark,
Suddenly flashing from moonglow lit.
Then the angel high on the topmost spire
Shimmered and smiled in her sweet way
As she looked at the toys by the dying fire,
Waiting for morning and Christmas Day:
The teddy bear of cinnamon plush,
The bright red sled, each nut-filled sack,
The bisque doll lovely with cheeks' pink blush,
Tea set, books, and a jumping jack,
Tiddlywinks, puzzles, some beads to string,
Small cast-iron stove, but best of all
The gifts that Santa Claus used to bring
Was the soft and cuddly old rag doll.
Then the moon slipped away over crusted snow,
The fire log snapped, and the wind song rang.
In such darkness the balsam stood long ago
While the herald angels softly sang.

THE GREAT CHRISTMAS TREE on the table bore many apples of
silver and of gold, and all of its branches were heavy with bud
and blossom, consisting of sugar almonds, many-tinted bon-
bons, and all sorts of things to eat.

Perhaps the prettiest thing about this wonder-tree, however,
was the fact that in all the recesses of its spreading branches hun-
dreds of little tapers descended like stars, inviting the children to
pluck its flowers and fruit.

—E. T. A. Hoffmann

Christmas on the Old Farm

Ann Silva

Only a few more days—and the sounds, the tastes, the smells, and the joys that they bring to the farm—remain before Christmas. Outside, in the frosty-cold farmyard, stands the old smokehouse, weathered a silver gray. Inside the smokehouse are the smells of Grandma's homemade soap, kept in the first room along with hoes, shovels, sickles, and kegs of nails. In the darkened room in the back are hams, sausages, and salted meats in crocks.

Inside the white frame walls of the farmhouse, hands large and small are busy cleaning and dusting and polishing everything in sight. Silver begins to gleam and sparkle in the gentle light of the fire. Syrup pitchers are full, and the pantry is stocked with apples, pies, cakes, and chocolate fudge loaded with nuts. And there are plenty of Grandma's homemade pickles—how we children love them!

In the parlor, the old pump organ is opened, decorated for the season with fresh-scented pine and holly boughs. The tree stands in the corner, trimmed with glitter and polished apples and oranges wrapped in tissue paper and tied with red ribbons. The tree will be lit—only on Christmas Eve, and only for a short while—by homemade candles. But we do not need the lights on the tree to tell us it is Christmas; its aroma, mingled with that of the bayberry candles, fills the room, and we know for certain that it is Christmastime on the old family farm.

Country Christmas

Elisabeth Weaver Winstead

Christmastime in the country—
What magic it is to be
Hanging wreaths of fragrant holly,
Bringing home the Christmas tree.

Handmade gifts with homespun flair,
Country dolls with braided hair,
Yarn stockings by the chimney hung,
On the doorstep, soft carols sung.

Sleigh bells jingling in the night,
Snowflakes falling, sparkling bright,

On frozen pond, ice-skating fun,
Red cheeks aglow on everyone.

Fruitcakes baking and holiday pie,
Cookies and eggnog for friends dropping by,
Plum pudding steaming in the pan,
Sweet, spicy smell of a gingerbread man.

All snuggled warmly in quilt-covered beds;
Wondrous dreams fill children's heads.
The countryside echoes a message of cheer:
Christmas peace and love in a joyous year.

Snow-covered woodpile in Bristol, New Hampshire.
Photograph by William H. Johnson

An Iowa Christmas

Paul Engle

Every Christmas should begin with the sound of bells; and when I was a child, mine always did. But they were sleigh bells, not church bells, for we lived in a part of Cedar Rapids, Iowa, where there were no churches. My bells were on my father's team of horses as he drove up to our horse-headed hitching post with the bobsled that would take us to celebrate Christmas on the family farm ten miles out in the country. My father would bring the team down Fifth Avenue at a smart trot, flicking his whip over the horses' rumps and making the bells double their light, thin jangling over the snow, whose radiance threw back a brilliance like the sound of bells.

There are no such departures anymore—the whole family piling into the bobsled with a foot of golden oat straw to lie in and heavy buffalo robes to lie under, the horses stamping the soft snow, and at every motion of their hoofs the bells jingling, jingling. . . .

There are no streets like those any more, the snow sensibly left on the road for the sake of sleighs and easy travel. We could hop off and ride the heavy runners as they made their hissing, tearing sound over the packed snow. And along the streets we met other horses, so that we moved from one set of bells to another, from the tiny tinkle of the individual bells on the shafts to the silver, leaping sound of the long strands hung over the harness. There would be an occasional brass-mounted automobile laboring on its narrow tires and, as often as not, pulled up the slippery hills by a horse, and we would pass it with a triumphant shout for an awkward nuisance which was obviously not here to stay. . . .

Near the low house on the hill, with oaks on one side and apple trees on the other, my father would stand up, flourish his whip, and bring the bobsled right up to the door of the house with a burst of speed.

There are no such arrivals any more: the harness bells ringing and clashing; the horses whinnying at the horse in the barn and receiving a great, trumpeting whinny in reply; the dogs leaping into the bobsled and burrowing under the buffalo robes; a squawking from the hen house; a yelling of "Whoa, whoa," at the excited horses; boy and girl cousins howling around the bobsled; and the descent into the snow with the Christmas basket carried by my mother.

While my mother and sisters went into the house, the team was unhitched and taken to the barn, to be covered with blankets and given a little grain. That winter odor of a barn is a wonderfully complex one, rich and warm and utterly unlike the smell of the same barn in summer. . . . It is a smell from strong and living things, and my father always said it was the secret of health, that it scoured out a man's lungs; and he would stand there, breathing deeply, one hand on a horse's rump, watching the steam come out from under the blankets as the team cooled down from their rapid trot up the lane. It gave him a better appetite, he argued, than plain fresh air, which was thin and had no body to it.

A barn with cattle and horses is the place to begin Christmas; after all, that's where the original event happened, and that same smell was the first air that the Christ Child breathed.

Barn in Kewaunee County, Wisconsin.
Photograph by Darryl R. Beers

The snow sparkled sharply outside the door,
And the house a bright mantle of icicles wore.
But the inside was warm with
the love that was there
With a spirit of giving and
wanting to share.
—JUNE R. COLLINS

Wreath of holly and Christmas cards. Photograph by Jessie Walker

With Your Card

Edith G. Schay

You sent a pine sprig with your card;
And right beyond my sunny yard
I see the North, far hills, tall pines,
Warm wishes from your hearth to mine.
Oh, tell me, did you really know
You sent me silver-scented snow,
Sent memories touched with tinsel-shine,
Sent Christmas in one sprig of pine?

Christmas Cards

Edna Jaques

How lovely are the sentiments
    Contained in Christmas cards,
As well as dear, heartwarming scenes
    Of snowy trees and yards.
They never change so very much,
    But who would want it so?
For Christmas seems to just belong
    To cedar trees and snow.

The greetings on a Christmas card
    Are precious as a gem,
Because old neighbors and old friends
    Send us their love with them—

Warming our hearts with loving words,
    Making us know that they
Are thinking of dear bygone times,
    Upon this Christmas Day.

A holly wreath, a little church,
    A lovely lighted door,
Some carol singers in the street,
    The windows of a store—
All these are part of Christmastime,
    Like cake and mistletoe,
Because a card arrived today
    And sort of told me so.

Caroling
Virginia Blanck Moore

There's no sweeter sound
Than carols sung
By a group of voices
Clear and young.
Akin to the angels
Of long ago,
The notes float out
O'er glistening snow.

And as the voices
Rise and blend,
The listener hopes
It shall never end—
This way of telling
A waiting earth
The age-old news
Of a Savior's birth.

A Joyful Christmas
Nadine Brothers Lybarger

The world is bright with Christmas lights—
Wherever did you see
A lovelier sight than shines tonight
From housefront, lawn, and tree?

The air is filled with melody:
Whenever did you hear
A sweeter sound, the world around,
Than these we hold so dear:

Familiar Christmas carols sung
With reverence in each word;
Soft bells in distant steeples rung
As though by angels stirred.

The world's alive with Christmas joy!
Come join the merry throng.
You'll find upon your lips a smile,
Within your heart, a song.

Carols to a Neighbor
Maurice W. Fogle

As long as friendly light
Glows out your windowpane,
A soft petition into night,
Another carol we will sing to you,
A Christmas Eve refrain.

As long as one candle burns
From out your windowsill
Through spatterfrost and ferns,
Another carol we will sing to you
Of peace and God's goodwill.

As long as we can see a star,
Radiant on your Christmas tree,
Spreading love and welcome far,
Another carol we will sing to you,
A promised Child's Nativity.

As long as a single lamp
Shows eagerness through windowframe
Of Magi march and shepherd tramp,
Another carol we will sing to you
And hymn His blessed name.

Christmas carol music. Photograph by Nancy Matthews

There Shall Be Music
Alice Leedy Mason

There shall be music, sweet and clear,
Calling the reverent worshipers near,
Telling the story in notes and in rhyme
Of the Child who was born at Christmastime.

There shall be music, soft and light,
A lullaby sung on a crisp winter night,
Sweetly angelic like the voices that told
Of the birth of a king to the shepherds of old.

There shall be music, deep and strong,
Filling the air with melodious song,
Resonant sounds of gladness that tend
To lift every heart to a grateful *amen!*

Christmas Carillon
Jean Hogan Dudley

The little bells of Christmas keep
Their faith against the tides of night;
To all awake and all asleep,
Chimes flow like drifts of silver light.

The age-old words our hearts supply,
As suddenly in awe again
We hear bright music fill the sky
For peace on earth, goodwill to men.

And though the night is shadowing
And stars are dim and high above,
The little bells of Christmas sing
Our faith in God's unending love.

The world's largest church organ, Passau Cathedral, Germany. Photograph from SuperStock

Candlelight
Brian F. King

Reluctant is the darkest night
To threaten bliss of candlelight;
For where the waxen tapers glow,
Grim, questing shadows dare not go.

Soft candlelight betokens cheer
That beckons when the dusk appears
And sends its gentle, golden beams
To set bright silverware agleam.

It bathes within its subtle fire
The household things of heart's desire.
Where scented candles bring delight,
Small children welcome stars of night.

And love is ever-present where
The charm of candlelight is there;
For living reaches heights sublime
When candles glow at twilight time.

Christmas Light
Virginia Blanck Moore

A tall red taper burns below
   a holly wreath. The crystal snow
   flings back the silver light
   of stars. Still is the night. . . .
And all the world recalls a birth,
An angel's song, and peace on earth.

A Christmas Moment
Cindi Swanson

I sit in the quiet solitude of the candlelit room,
   so softly scented with Christmas pine and peppermint;
Through the window smeared the day before
   with a small wet, mittened hand,
I watch the quietly falling snow, gently blanketing the ground with white,
   like a grandmother's comforter,
Each knot carefully tied with love and warmth.

A softly lit alcove. Photograph by Jessie Walker

It's Coming Christmastime

Mary Reas

When you feel that bit of friendliness
Where before it wasn't found,
When you see a warmth within a smile
Where once there was a frown,
You know at once it's almost here;
It reflects in song and rhyme,
And love is felt throughout the world:
It's coming Christmastime.

When you're shoved and jostled in a crowd
And your patience grows quite thin,
Someone might whisper, "Pardon me,"
And you'll feel that glow again.
There's something magic happening;
No mistaking in the sign.
When folks begin to love again,
It's coming Christmastime.

You'd love to give to everyone,
No matter what the cost.
You think of all the friends you've made
And regret the ones you've lost.
The wind is cold against your skin,
Yet all is warm inside
Because the world's in love again:
It's coming Christmastime.

Dearer than memory, brighter than expectation is the ever returning *now* of Christmas. Why else, each time we greet its return, should happiness ring out in us like a peal of bells?

—ELIZABETH BOWEN

Stores in Wiscasset, Maine, decorated for the holidays. Photograph by William H. Johnson

Come to the Manger
Wendy Dunham

When I was young, the first day of every December marked a yearly event for our family. This was the day we chose our Christmas tree. Early in the morning, Dad would call to us, "Everyone ready? Let's go cut down the tree!"

After what seemed like a drive that would never end, Dad finally shouted, "We're here! And look, Mr. Nicoles has the same sign he had when I was a kid and we came to cut down our tree."

CHRISTMAS TREES
3 ACRES—U-CUT

Mr. Nicoles came out on the porch to greet us. When he and Dad began to reminisce about past visits, I sneaked away to the front yard. Standing there was a wooden, life-sized Nativity scene, hand-carved years ago by Mr. Nicoles. When I knelt before the manger, I was transported back to Bethlehem. I ran my hand along the manger's wood and it seemed to be worn smooth from sheep and cattle. I smelled the frankincense and touched the gold. I saw Joseph stroke Mary's head as she watched over Baby Jesus. And I heard the angels sing.

"Come on, Wendy," Dad called. "It's time to pick out the Christmas tree."

Reluctantly I joined the rest of the family, but I longed to stay in Bethlehem.

"We've got a lot of land to cover," Dad said. "Remember, we don't have to get the first tree we see."

Along the way, each of us tried to convince Dad that we had found the perfect tree. We knew that the sooner we made a choice, the sooner we could begin the long ride home.

Mother knew when her children had had enough. "Dear," she said to Dad, "don't you think this one will do? It's lovely, tall, full, and the needles are just the right length."

After Dad had cut down our choice, we took turns dragging the ten-foot tree through nearly a mile of deep snow. When we reached the house, Dad tied the tree to the top of the car.

I quietly returned to the manger. As I knelt there, I realized that I was not alone. Mr. Nicoles was standing behind me.

"I can always find you at the manger," he said.

I stood and turned to face him. "I like it here."

"So do I," he said softly.

We stood, side by side, and looked out across the blanket of snow that covered the farm. I noticed a trail of freshly made footprints in the middle of the yard. A deep trench ran behind the footprints, as if something had been dragged across the snow.

"Whose footprints are those going to your Christmas tree sign?" I asked.

"They're mine," Mr. Nicoles responded.

Puzzled, I said, "But you opened your farm the day after Thanksgiving."

Mr. Nicoles bent low and whispered, "Can you keep a secret? I put the sign out this morning, just as I have for the past four years. When your family heads home, I'll take it down."

"Why? I don't understand."

"I have grown too old to run the farm, but I know how much this place means to your father."

He smiled. "I look forward to seeing your family every December first."

"And the manger?"

"Oh, I set that out for the entire season. I like to kneel before the manger too; and when I do, I can hear the angels sing."

More than fifty years have passed since that day. Mr. Nicoles continued to open his farm on December first for three more years until his health prevented the ritual.

Now, I walk through the snow to my own front yard and to the hand-carved Nativity scene: a bequest from Mr. Nicoles. Once again, as I kneel before the manger, I am transported back to Bethlehem; and I forget about the cards waiting to be addressed, the baking that must be done, and the gifts still to be bought. For there, before the manger, I hear the angels sing.

Hemlocks in Stanley Park, Vancouver, British Columbia. Photograph by Terry Donnelly

Nature's Ornaments

Lansing Christman

I am a fireside dreamer this Christmastime. The skies are the windows of my home; the land is the carpet. The frost and sun, the snow and ice, and the moon and stars are the ornaments.

These are the shortest days of the year, and dusk turns quickly into darkness. On these December nights, the stars come early; their glitter fills the skies with twinkling lights. Looking up from my doorstep, I can see the branches of the trees forming intricate silhouettes against the glow of the moon.

Winter dresses the outdoors in wondrous icy splendor. The fingers of the snow weave the finest of laces, gowning every evergreen and draping ribbons of white over the boles and branches of the hickories and oaks. The gleaming, starry flakes shine like diamonds in the glow of a mellow moon.

On Christmas morning, the sun-brilliant frost slips silvered jewels on every blade of grass and also silvers the bloom of the dandelion that pushes up through the grass like a nugget of gold. The frost shapes the gems, the snow weaves the lace, the ice strings the purest pearls, and the glowing moon loops the slopes in the richest jewels. I have yet to see a hand that can decorate a tree, a window, or a room in such beauty and intricacy; I have yet to see fingers that can weave such finery of lace.

From my window, I can see the silver and gold, the red and the blue, and all the dazzling and sparkling colors on a tree glowing in all its beauty for the holiday. Outside my door are bells, tinsels, gems.

Yes, I am a fireside dreamer this holy night. I look up to the skies and the twinkling stars; they are the lamps in the windows of my world, a world designed by God.

Snow-tipped ponderosa pine trees in Freemont National Forest, Oregon. Photograph by Dennis Frates

It's Time Again

Vera Laurel Hoffman

The hills are bright with soft new snow;
And in the glen a space below,
The church stands glowing in the light
That creeps across the land tonight.
The footsteps through the fallen snow
Wind down a hill, and on they go
To stop before the great church door
While organ music starts to pour
Out o'er the twilight soft and clear—
Another Christmastime is here.

The steeple's gold is like a sign
Aflame to welcome Christmastime;
Its windows gleam in orange and blue,
Recalling ancient scenes we knew.
The people come from near and far,
As years ago a shining star
Shone from the heavens, guiding men
To the small town of Bethlehem.
Now church bells ring out clear and call
To others as the shadows fall.

'Tis time to kneel and praise and sing
Hosannas to the newborn King!

So all the stars of the midnight
    which compass us round
Shall see a strange glory
    and hear a strange sound
And cry, "Look! the earth
    is aflame with delight;
O sons of the morning,
    rejoice at the sight."
Everywhere, everywhere,
    Christmas tonight!

—PHILLIPS BROOKS

Congregational Church, Amherst, New Hampshire.
Photograph by William H. Johnson

A Very Young Angel

Pat Leonard

John was almost five years old that Christmas. He did not have a part in the school Christmas pageant but was just one of the many children in the kindergarten class choir.

As the children gathered in the assembly room at school for the program, the teachers were busy with preparations and the costumes of those chosen to be Mary and Joseph and the angels, shepherds, and wise men. No one noticed a little boy go out the door into the hall.

John had heard the baby! There was to be a baby—he knew that. And he had heard him. Down the dark hall was the way he had to go. As he walked, John wondered why God didn't send the star, and then he remembered. The star wasn't for him. It was really for the shepherds and the wise men, and he wasn't anybody important like that. He'd have to be very brave and go alone to find the baby. He turned the corner cautiously.

At the far end of the hall, John saw a light

coming from a doorway. Then he heard the baby's cry more clearly. He knew then where to go.

Mary Meadowcraft knelt beside the brown beanbag chair her husband, Joe, had brought to school for his sixth-grade reading corner as she put young Jeffrey down to rest. He was normally a contented baby. Had she known he would cry like this, she would have stayed at home with him instead of coming to school with Joe to see the pageant.

The sudden presence of so many eager children must have frightened Jeffrey, for he began crying almost immediately and would not be stilled. At least the program would not be long. Mary had decided to wait here in Joe's classroom with the baby so his crying would not disturb anyone.

Suddenly Mary was startled to hear a little voice questioning, "Are you Mary?"

"Why, yes, I am," she answered with amazement. "Do I know you?"

"I came to see your baby," said John. "I didn't know He ever cried like that," he added softly.

"Jeffrey is just frightened to be in a strange place."

"Hi," John said as he too knelt down beside the baby. "I'm John. I'm not a wise man or anything, but they couldn't come."

HE IS BORN. *Painting by Frances Hook*

The baby stopped crying immediately and turned to look at John. Mary remained perfectly still, her mouth drawn into an astonished "Oh!"

"I forgot to bring you something, little Jeffrey Jesus." Then John smiled. "I know what I can give you. I'll sing you a song that we've been practicing. I know all the words!"

By now John's parents had come searching for him. They were stopped in the doorway, however, by the sight of Mary and her baby listening to John's gift of song:

> *Bless all the dear children*
> *In Your tender care*
> *And take us to Heaven*
> *To live with You there.*

The baby beamed at the singing child, while the three adults, their hearts full of wonder, saw a glimpse of a very young angel that night.

A Child's Nativity
Eileen Spinelli

Star cut from a piece of tin,
Flannel camel, cardboard inn,
Stable built in someone's shed,
Old desk drawer a manger bed.
Cotton-bearded, bathrobed kings,
Angels wearing paper wings,
Joseph—just a boy named Jim;
In math class I sit next to him.
Shepherd's staff a broken rake;
Incense, gold, and myrrh—all fake.

Nothing real except the part
When Christmas joy
Fills every heart.

A Night Like This
Reginald Holmes

This Christmas Eve the old red barn is filled
To topmost beam with crisp alfalfa hay.
The earth is locked in winter's icy grasp,
But here is the fragrance of a bright June day.

An air of hushed expectancy prevails;
The evening star hangs low in moonlit skies;
A newborn calf stands at its mother's side
And views a newfound world with wondering eyes.

The sheep have piled their fleecy whiteness here
To form a contrast with the drab gray walls;
They raise their heads and silently protest,
As horses softly neigh in nearby stalls.

No man alive dare say their vision soars
No higher than those wooded pasture bars.
Who knows, but long ago they scanned the skies
And saw the brilliance of that star of stars.

But this I surely know—a miracle
Will never be to them a strange new thing;
For on a night like this, in Bethlehem,
Their forebears watched the advent of the King.

Bethlehem of Judea
Author Unknown

A little child,
    A shining star,
A stable rude,
    The door ajar.

Yet in that place,
    So crude, forlorn,
The Hope of all
    The world was born.

Gambrel barn in Charlemont, Massachusetts.
Photograph by William H. Johnson

Simplicity

Hal Borland

Not the least of the wonders we celebrate today was the simplicity surrounding the Birth itself. A carpenter named Joseph went with his young wife up from Nazareth to Bethlehem, the town of his fathers, to enroll for taxation as the governing Romans had ordered. Joseph and Mary arrived late and weary to find that the inn was crowded; so they took shelter in the stable with other latecomers. Second-best, but humble travelers could not choose. It was shelter. And there in the stable the Child was born.

Thus the simple beginnings. Add the shepherds on the night hills, the appearance of the angel, their journey to the stable, and it still remains one of the least adorned of all the great stories we cherish. It is as simple as was the Man Himself and His teaching. As simple as the Sermon on the Mount, which still stands, in its essentials, as the summary of the belief of free men of goodwill everywhere.

There were the night hills with the little town among them. And in a stable there was born One who came to speak to multitudes about freedom and justice and fundamental right. One who spoke in a simple tongue, in terms of the beasts of the land, the birds of the air, the lilies of the fields, and man's responsibility to man. The kings and captains were marching up and down the land, in full panoply, even as He was being born. But it is His simple words that endure, not theirs; and it is the Birth at the stable that we solemnly commemorate, not the gathering at the crowded inn.

THE EVENING GLOW. *Painting by Joseph Farquharson*

The Oxen
Thomas Hardy

Christmas Eve, and twelve of the clock,
    "Now they are all on their knees,"
An elder said as we sat in a flock
    By the embers in hearthside ease.

We pictured the meek, mild creatures where
    They dwelt in their strawy pen;
Nor did it occur to one of us there
    To doubt they were kneeling then.

So fair a fancy few would weave
    In these years! Yet, I feel,
If someone said on Christmas Eve,
    "Come; see the oxen kneel,

"In the lonely barton by yonder coomb
    Our childhood used to know,"
I should go with him in the gloom,
    Hoping it might be so.

The Restless Doves
Ralph W. Seager

Only the doves were restless now;
The ewes were quiet, and the peaceful cow
Had settled down in the straw again;
And goats lay drowsy in their pen.

Yet higher up about the gable,
Above the manger and the stable,

Doves could sense the rushing flight
That moved the strange winds in this night.

There was within these feathered things
A kinship with all other wings,
And doves would know that Christmas Day
Was just an angel's wing away.

Sheep peering through a snowfall. Photograph by Dennis Frates

ℬETHLEHEM
Luke 2:1–7

And it came to pass in those days, that there went out a decree from Caesar Augustus, that all the world should be taxed. (And this taxing was first made when Cyrenius was governor of Syria.) And all went to be taxed, every one into his own city.

And Joseph also went up from Galilee, out of the city of Nazareth, into Judaea, unto the city of David, which is called Bethlehem; (because he was of the house and lineage of David:) To be taxed with Mary his espoused wife, being great with child.

And so it was, that, while they were there, the days were accomplished that she should be delivered.

And she brought forth her firstborn son, and wrapped him in swaddling clothes, and laid him in a manger; because there was no room for them in the inn.

THE ADORATION. *Painting by Gerrit van Honthorst*

THE ANGELS
Luke 2:8–14

And there were in the same country shepherds abiding in the field, keeping watch over their flock by night.

And, lo, the angel of the Lord came upon them, and the glory of the Lord shone round about them: and they were sore afraid.

And the angel said unto them, Fear not: for, behold, I bring you good tidings of great joy, which shall be to all people.

For unto you is born this day in the city of David a Saviour, which is Christ the Lord.

And this shall be a sign unto you; Ye shall find the babe wrapped in swaddling clothes, lying in a manger.

And suddenly there was with the angel a multitude of the heavenly host praising God, and saying,

Glory to God in the highest, and on earth peace, good will toward men.

ANGEL APPEARING TO SHEPHERDS. *Painting by Nicolas Berchem*

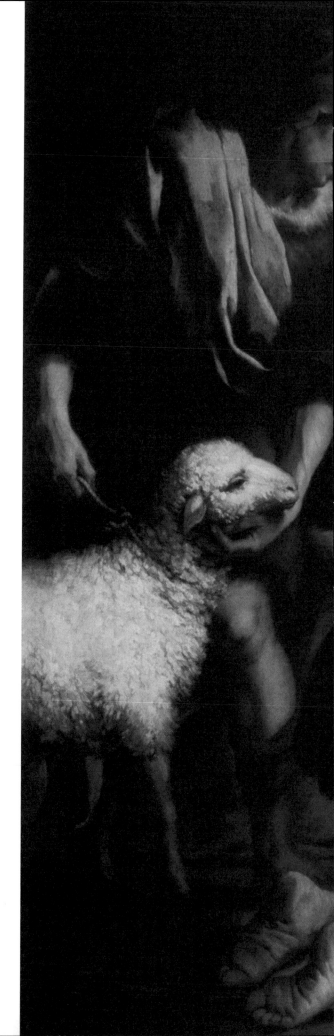

THE MANGER
Luke 2:15–19

And it came to pass, as the angels were gone away from them into heaven, the shepherds said one to another, Let us now go even unto Bethlehem, and see this thing which is come to pass, which the Lord hath made known unto us.

And they came with haste, and found Mary, and Joseph, and the babe lying in a manger.

And when they had seen it, they made known abroad the saying which was told them concerning this child.

And all they that heard it wondered at those things which were told them by the shepherds.

But Mary kept all these things, and pondered them in her heart.

And the shepherds returned, glorifying and praising God for all the things that they had heard and seen, as it was told unto them.

THE ADORATION OF THE SHEPHERDS.
Painting by Bartolome Esteban Murillo

The Voice of the Christ-Child
Phillips Brooks

The earth has grown old with its burden of care,
But at Christmas it always is young;
The heart of the jewel burns lustrous and fair,
And its soul full of music breaks forth on the air,
When the song of the angels is sung.

It is coming, old earth, it is coming tonight!
On snowflakes which covered thy sod,
The feet of the Christ-child fall gently and white,
And the voice of the Christ-child tells out with delight
That mankind are the children of God.

On the sad and the lonely, the wretched and poor,
The voice of the Christ-child shall fall;
And to every blind wanderer opens the door
Of a hope which he dared not to dream of before,
With a sunshine of welcome for all.

The feet of the humblest may walk in the field
Where the feet of the holiest have trod—
This, this is the marvel to mortals revealed,
When the silvery trumpets of Christmas have pealed,
That mankind are the children of God.

Christmas
Faith Baldwin

The snow is full of silver light
Spilled from the heavens' tilted cup;
And on this holy, tranquil night,
The eyes of men are lifted up
To see the promise written fair,
The hope of peace for all on earth,
And hear the singing bells declare
The marvel of the dear Christ's birth.

The way from year to year is long
And though the road be dark so far,
Bright is the manger, sweet the song;
The steeple rises to the Star.

A snow-covered road in Deschutes National Forest, Oregon. Photograph by Dennis Frates

The Christmas Gift

Pamela Kennedy

Our family really enjoys Christmas gifts. We like buying them, wrapping them, hiding them, putting them under the tree, anticipating them, and especially opening them. Family gifts are placed under the tree and stockings are stuffed on Christmas Eve.

When the children were young, my husband and I bustled around after the kids were in bed, bringing out the wrapped gifts from their hiding places to arrange them under the fragrant fir branches. Then we carefully stuffed each home-made stocking with smaller items and set them at the base of the tree as well.

When the children awoke on Christmas morning, no one could venture forth to look at the tree until Mom and Dad were up, dressed, and ready to go. I always slipped out to turn on the tree lights and the Christmas music and start a pot of coffee, but the kids remained behind in our room with their father, who took delight in spending a few extra minutes shaving or combing his hair on Christmas morning, while the kids squirmed on our bed, pleading, "WHEN are you going to be done, Dad?"

When the anticipation peaked, my husband led our anxious offspring out to view their Christmas bounty. We always took delight in their wide eyes and grins as they carefully examined the colorful packages and fur-trimmed stockings. Then the oldest child passed the stuffed Christmas socks around, and we began opening their contents.

We always take turns unwrapping presents. Each person opens one thing, then the next person opens one, and so forth around the family circle until all the stockings are emptied. At some point several years ago, our older son decided to try to guess what was in each stocking gift before opening it. None of us can figure out how he does it, but his accuracy average is currently up to about ninety percent!

When the stocking gifts are all opened and deposited into individual bags, we break for our traditional breakfast of Julekake, a Scandinavian holiday sweetbread traditionally baked during the holidays in my husband's family for over sixty years.

After breakfast, we re-gather around the tree and begin opening our packages, again one at a time, so each person has an opportunity not only to discover and appreciate the gift, but to also appropriately thank the giver. Often there are stories to tell of how the gift was chosen, or a contented sigh of relief when the giver hears, "Oh, I really like this. Thanks so much!" Our Christmas mornings are leisurely and long, and we relish the closeness we feel as each member of the family enjoys the opportunity to give and to receive.

The ancient Scriptures remind us that the gift of the Savior had been planned for centuries.

I know that gift giving has become a commercialized frenzy and, for many, a burden. I always cringe as I'm driving home from the mall, car filled with bags of Christmas presents, or staying up late to put the finishing touches on a homemade gift and someone on the radio enjoins

me to "forget the hustle and bustle of the holiday season and get back to the real meaning of Christmas." I want to counter, "but for me and my family, gift giving actually is all about the real meaning of Christmas." I think our sharing of gifts at Christmas is delightful reminder, if only a pale reflection, of what God did on that very first Christmas a couple thousand years ago.

The ancient Scriptures remind us that the gift of the Savior had been planned for centuries. Prophets had predicted His coming, but no one knew where or when the Gift would be given. The secret was hidden in the heart of God, waiting for just the right moment, for just the right amount of anticipation, for just the right degree of need. Then, "in the fullness of time," the Gift was wrapped tenderly in flesh and delivered to the world on a starlit night in Bethlehem. Embraced in the arms of a family, the heavenly Present was received with joy and gratitude while shepherds and angels wondered at the lavish outpouring of the Creator's love. I believe the Giver delighted in knowing just what His beloved children needed that first Christmas and took divine pleasure in receiving their heartfelt thanks.

The amazing thing about God's Christmas Gift, however, is that it never wears out, gets old, or goes out of style. Every generation, every individual, has the opportunity to receive it anew, and not only at Christmas, but also every day of every year. Our gifts to our loved ones are just temporary reminders of how much we care for and value them. The generosity of our Heavenly Father is unending. Morning by morning we are surprised by the gifts of God. The smile of a dear friend, the song of a solitary bird, every breath and heartbeat, are all expressions of His abundant love. As the beautiful carol reminds us: "How silently, how silently the wondrous gift is giv'n! So God imparts to human hearts the blessings of His heav'n."

Chickadee perched on a branch. Photograph from Jupiter Images

The Way to See Christmas
Ruth Carter

The way to see Christmas is through a child's eyes,
As he opens with rapture some hidden surprise;
As he looks at the tree with its light blue and gold;
As he climbs on your lap knowing arms will enfold.
Someone plays Christmas carols; you listen; you rock;
Save the music, no sound but the ticktock of clock.

In spite of your worries, in spite of your grief,
'Tis the child and his wonder, his trusting belief,
Renewing your faith in that Child long ago,
Reflected in your child, God's gift to bestow.
Rock away, rock away, loveliness keep
Of the child on your shoulder, fallen asleep.

So the way to see Christmas, if you would be wise,
Is to share it with children; see joy in their eyes.
For the world is a weary world; troubles increase.
But the child who is loved, it is he who has peace.

*It is Christmas every time
you let God love others
through you. . . .*
—MOTHER THERESA

The Perfect Gift
Phyllis M. Flaig

I do not ask for lavish gifts
Nor satin gowns to wear;
I have no need for jeweled combs
Or flowers in my hair.
I only ask on Christmas Day
To find when I arise,
That I may see the world again
With a child's unclouded eyes.

*Children gazing at a Christmas tree.
Photograph by Rosemary Weller/Getty Images*

"From Our Earliest Christmas Times…"

Eudora Welty

From our earliest Christmas times, Santa Claus brought us toys that instruct boys and girls (separately) how to build things—stone blocks cut to the castle-building style, Tinkertoys, and erector sets. Daddy made for us himself elaborate kites that needed to be taken miles out of town to a pasture long enough (and my father was not afraid of horses and cows watching) for him to run with and get up on a long cord to which my mother held the spindle, and then we children were given it to hold, tugging like something alive at our hands. They were beautiful, sound, shapely box kites, smelling delicately of office glue for their entire short lives.

And of course, as soon as the boys attained anywhere near the right age, there was an electric train, the engine with its pea-sized working headlight, its stations, its bridges, and its tunnel, which blocked off all other traffic in the upstairs hall. Even from downstairs, and through the cries of excited children, the elegant rush and click of the train could be heard through the ceiling, running around and around its figure eight.

All of this, but especially the train, represents my father's fondest beliefs—in progress, in the future. With these gifts, he was preparing his children.

Christmas tree with toys.
Photograph by Daniel Dempster

An Old-Fashioned Christmas

Adam N. Reiter

Away with a dash and jingling bells
    In a two-horse cutter sleigh,
The children are off to Grandmother's house
    For an old-style Christmas Day.
There's sparkling beauty o'er valley and hill
    And a nip in the frosty air;
There's hearty cheer in the neighbor's hail
    And gladness everywhere.

A grand old place is Grandmother's house,
    Massive and rambling and low,
Nestled and hid in the lee of a hill
    And wrapped in a blanket of snow.
Down the lane and over the bridge,
    Then on to the opened door;
Greeted by Rover's welcome bark
    And those who've arrived before.

Grandmother's kitchen is all aglow
    With a friendly cheer of its own,
With singing kettle and glowing hearth
    That beams with the warmth of home.
Grandfather sits in his easy chair
    With his favorite pipe alight;
The clan has gathered; the children are home;
    It's Christmas and "all is right!"

Grandmother's table is bountifully laid
    With good things for young and old;
The monstrous turkey is done to a turn,
    And the pies a sight to behold.

There's a tiny twinkle in Grandfather's eye,
    And Grandmother's smiling too—
Ah, that was a Christmas beyond compare,
    That we of a past day knew.

Dinner is done, and the scene is changed
    For one of richer content:
The parlor boasts of a glittering tree,
    And hours are happily spent
In merry chat and holiday fest.
    There's a gift for each one there—
'Twas a wonderful day at the old homeplace,
    And a measure of joy to spare.
It seems we basked in radiant charm,
    Perchance from a golden ray,
Far-flung from grim Judean hills
    In token of Christmas Day.
Reflected, too, in smiling face
    Is the glow of an inner light,
As voices near to the organ tell
    Of a "Silent, Holy Night."

But all good things must come to an end;
    The afternoon sun is low.
The horses are hitched to the creaking sleigh,
    For it's time for the children to go.
Chores await, and the long road looms;
    We're off in the gathering gloom,
With prancing feet and a flourish of bells,
    Over the hills, back home.

A pine table set for Christmas dinner with Royal Staffordshire china.
Photograph by Jessie Walker

Christmas Long Ago

Alice Kennelly Roberts

Remember Christmas long ago
When all the world outside was snow?
When every sound that sleepless night
Envisioned sleigh and reindeer's flight?
And when at last the morning dawned,
We found some angel's magic wand
Had touched the tree and hanging socks
And scattered many a beribboned box?

Excited cries and shouts of glee
Went whirling round the Christmas tree,
Until the turkey, roasted brown,
Bade every hungry child sit down,
While Father prayed a Christmas prayer
For all the family gathered there
And asked a blessing on our land;
We had to grow to understand.

Then back to all the Christmas joys
That came the way of girls and boys,
'Mid holly wreaths and tinseled star
And songs of carolers drifting far;
So drifted we to dreams that night,
Content that all the world was bright,
Convinced that He whose star still shone
Had claimed us for His very own.

O blessed days of peace and prayer,
When happy childhood knew no care,
When all of life before us lay
And worlds were ours on Christmas Day!
How like a snowball in the sun,
The years have vanished one by one.
How like the hills which skyward climb,
The truths we learned have conquered time!

SHOVELING OUT. *Painting by Robert Duncan*

There'll Always Be Christmas

Edna Jaques

There'll always be Christmas
As long as a light
Glows in the window
To guide folks at night.
As long as a star
In the heavens above
Keeps shining down,
There'll be Christmas and love.

There'll always be Christmas
As long as a tree
Grows on a hilltop,
As long as the sea
Breaks into foam
On a white pebbled beach,
As long as there's laughter
And beautiful speech.

There'll always be Christmas
As long as a street
Gives back the echo
Of homeward-bound feet,
And children with mittens
And warm winter clothes
Have bright eyes that sparkle
And cheeks like a rose

There'll always be Christmas
With holly and snow
And church bells that ring
In the valley below,
Shop windows lit,
And doorways ajar,
And over the housetops
A glint of a star,

The cavernous length
Of a stocking to fill,
A wreath on the window,
A light on a hill,
The song of the angels,
And, over again,
The beautiful message—
Goodwill among men.

ISBN 0-8249-1311-6

Published by Ideals Publications, a Guideposts Company
535 Metroplex Drive, Suite 250, Nashville, Tennessee 37211
www.idealsbooks.com

Cover photograph: A holiday wreath. Photograph by Larry LeFever/Grant Heilman
Inside front cover: HOLIDAY LIGHT. Painting from Ideals Publications
Inside back cover: THE YOUNGEST CAROLERS. Painting by George Hinke

ACKNOWLEDGMENTS

BALDWIN, FAITH. "Christmas" from Many Windows, Seasons of the Heart. Copyright © 1958 by Faith Baldwin Cuthrell, and from The Christian Herald, December 1949. Used by permission of Harold Ober Associates. BORLAND, HAL. "Simplicity" from This Hill, This Valley. Copyright © 1957 by Hal Borland, renewed © 1985 by Barbara Dodge Borland. Used by permission of Frances Collin, Literary Agent. CARTER, RUTH. "The Way to See Christmas." Originally published in the P. E. O. Record. Used here without objection. CHRISTMAN, LANSING. "Nature's Ornaments." Used by permission of Gayle McCants for the Estate of Lansing Christman. ENGLE, PAUL. "An Iowa Christmas" from A Prairie Christmas. Copyright © 1960 by Paul Engle. Used by permission of Hualing Nieh Engle. FIELD, RUTH B. "The Best Gift of All." Used by permission of Natalie Field Bevis. GUEST, EDGAR A. "Christmas Comes But Once a Year." Used by permission of M. Henry Sobell, III. HOLMES, MARJORIE. "Come Home With Me for Coffee" from The Evening Star Newspaper Company and At Christmas the Heart Goes Home. Doubleday, 1991. Used by permission of Dystel & Goderich Literary Management. HOLMES, REGINALD. "A Night Like This." Used by permission of Shirley A. Radwick. HOOVER, DAN A. "Homecoming Hearts." Used by permission of Carole Hoover Allen. JAQUES, EDNA. "There'll Always Be Christmas" from Ideals 1959, and "Christmas Cards" from The Golden Road by Edna Jaques. Copyright © 1953. Thomas Allen Ltd. Used by permission of Louise Bonnell. KRONSCHNABEL, DARLENE. "Christmas Baking" from Seasons in a Country Kitchen Cookbook. Copyright © 2005 by the author. Used by permission of Jones Books, Madison, WI. SANDERS, DORI. "Christmas Decorations," from Southern Christmas. Published by Hill Street Press, Athens, GA, 1998. WELTY, EUDORA. "From Our Earliest Christmas Times..." from One Writer's Beginnings. Copyright © 1983, 1984 by Eudora Welty. Published by Harvard University Press, Cambridge, Mass. Our sincere thanks to the following authors or their heirs, some of whom we were unable to locate, for material submitted or previously used in Ideals publications: June R. Collins, Jean Hogan Dudley, Wendy Dunham, Phyllis M. Flaig, Gladys Harp, Vera Laurel Hoffman, Roy Z. Kemp, Pamela Kennedy, Brian F. King, Pat Leonard, Nadine Brothers Lybarger, Alice Leedy Mason, Virginia Blanck Moore, Lon Myruski, Agnes M. Pharo, Lolita Pinney, Mary Reas, Adam N. Reiter, Alice Kennelly Roberts, Edith G. Schay, Ralph W. Seager, Ann Silva, Eileen Spinelli, Cynthia Swanson, Ruth H. Underhill, Elisabeth Weaver Winstead, Laura Hope Wood. Every effort has been made to establish ownership and use of each selection in this book. If contacted, the publisher will be pleased to rectify any inadvertent errors or omissions in subsequent reprints.